I0464791

Don't Let THE MAN Keep You Down

How To Successfully Start and Operate Your Own Business

©2014 William H. Joiner, Jr.

All rights reserved. No part of this publication may be reproduced or used in any form or by any means, graphic, electronic or mechanical, including photocopying, recording, taping, or information and retrieval systems without written permission of the publisher.

Edited by Missy Brewer

Book design by Michael Campbell, MCWriting.com

Cover design by Bryan Gehrke, MyCoverDesigner.com

ISBN: 978-1505630688

For more information visit www.williamjoinerauthor.com

DON'T LET THE MAN KEEP YOU DOWN

How To Successfully Start and Operate Your Own Business

WILLIAM H. JOINER, JR.

CONTENTS

Introduction

. . . .

WARNING!

There will be instances in this book where it will appear that I'm trying to talk you out of going into business for yourself. Nothing could be further from the truth. The purpose of this book is to provide information, **NOT** to hype you up about ridiculous notions of *"FOLLOW MY SIMPLE PLAN AND MAKE MILLIONS!"*

I know of plenty of books that make that type of outrageous claim in an attempt to sell books. I want you to be aware of the problems and pitfalls of starting and operating your business so you can make an informed decision about whether you are suited to starting a business.

• • •

So, you want to start, operate or expand your own business? Great! But first, let's take an in-depth look at your motivation and qualifications to do so.

Are you qualified?

Are you sick and tired of office politics? The aggravation of an idiotic or inept supervisor? The lack of rewards—both short and long term—in your current job? A great alternative may be to start your own business and be your own boss. But before you do, let's take a harder look at what it actually takes to make that leap of faith. The grass may not be greener over this particular fence.

Is your personality suited to having your own business? Owning your own business requires the ability to bounce back from the yo-yo-ing circumstances of "chicken one day, feathers the next" that is part of the experience of being an entrepreneur. Is your outlook on life one of *the-glass-is-half-full*, or are you a *glass-is-half-empty* type? If you automatically assume the worst, owning your own business may not be right for you.

An entrepreneur is a person who organizes and operates a business or businesses, taking on greater than normal financial risks to do so. With greater risks comes the potential for greater rewards.

Not being suited for the entrepreneurial lifestyle is not an indictment of who you are. God gave us all different personalities. Some folks are suited for it, some are not. Before starting this journey, be honest with yourself whether this is for you.

To a certain extent, entrepreneurs are born with:

✓ a driving passion for something

✓ the ability to see a better way of doing something

✓ problem-solving ability

✓ self-motivation

✓ the capacity to organize themselves

✓ a desire to help others

✓ confidence

✓ a dread of working for someone else

✓ a desire to make a name for themselves

✓ a tireless work ethic

✓ the ability to see potential

✓ a desire to set your own schedule

✓ creativity

✓ the ability to multitask

✓ a lack of fear of failure

✓ being a thrill-seeker

Most people possess some of these characteristics. The more of them you have, the better suited you are to being an entrepreneur.

I cannot guarantee your success. I can guarantee you that you will be tested. Your ability to solve problems under changing circumstances will have a great deal to do with whether you are successful.

Can you focus on the task in front of you, with the alligators of day-to-day problems nipping at your rear? Can you create order out of chaos? Can you still be persistent when everything you've tried has left you with an empty sack? Can you commit to your business behind only God, family and friends?

Every stage of business comes with its own set of problems, from the kitchen table office of the smallest of businesses to the boardroom of the largest of corporations. Problems must be solved for any business to survive and thrive, regardless of size.

Your decision to start your own business is not made in a vacuum. It involves your family and possibly your friends. Your family and friends may not encourage you. They may think you have lost your mind. If you are convinced you are right, it sometimes takes courage to go against the well-meaning opinions of family and friends to *play it safe* and stay with the status quo (the devil you know versus the devil you don't know).

For me, the thrill of being alive in a business sense is an adrenaline rush. I love being the captain (underneath God of course) of my own fate.

I once went on a bear hunt in Alaska. While there, I shot a bear but he disappeared in cover so thick I had to crawl on my hands and knees with only a pistol to recover him. Since I'm here to write about it, you know I survived, but during that tense stalk, every cell in my body was alive and fully alert. In fact, I have never felt more alive in my entire life!

The thrill of owning your own business can be intoxicating, but eventually that feeling wears off. Then begins the real part of making your business work: the day-to-day grind of operations. If you don't have the focus, persistence and commitment for that grind, your business won't be a success.

Entrepreneurs are also competitive. To them, business is a giant game, with money keeping the score. A successful business owner doesn't shrink when it comes time to compete in the marketplace. The marketplace of trade and commerce is the biggest game in the world. Competition is fierce, but inspiration and passion, backed up by know-how, can help you come out on the winning side.

At some point, it will be time to make your decision. You can practice swimming on dry land, but there's no substitute for getting in the water. You will probably have a mental tug-of-war with the powerful force of hope on one side and the equally powerful force of doubt and fear on the other side, trying to hinder you from going forward. You will have to decide. Are you in or are you out?

Why this book?

. . . .

Advice is plentiful and it is usually free. Sometimes you don't even have to ask for it. It is just given to you. With all this free advice available, why pay good money (albeit not much) for my advice in this book? Why is my advice any more valuable than anyone else's?

I started in business for myself 47 years ago, beginning when I was nineteen years old. I have birthed businesses in construction, real estate, insurance, ranching, oil and gas, international fuel, gold and silver trading, gyms and animal training. A more complete description of my background and history can be found in my book, *American Entrepreneur: an autobiography*. The eBook format will set you back a whopping 99 cents, the paperback $9.99.

All of my books can be found on my website:

www.williamjoinerauthor.com

It starts with a sale

. . . .

If you are suited to be an entrepreneur, it is an exhilarating life filled with satisfaction and a sense of the accomplishment of building something from nothing.

The single biggest piece of advice that I can give you is *EVERY* business begins with a *SALE*. It's really very simple: if you don't have a sale, you don't have a business. If you can't embrace being a salesperson, you are not suited to owning your own business. If you have your own business, you *WILL* be selling something; goods, services, and last but not least, yourself.

The next biggest piece of advice is find something you are passionate about. If you choose a business just based on financial rewards, you *WILL* eventually burn out and hate it as much as you do your current job. I will not make suggestions of different businesses that you can choose from because I don't know where your heart is. Only you can follow your heartfelt interests. The only hint I can give you is I don't think I ever had a hobby that I didn't turn into a business.

America is famous for success stories by individuals who pulled themselves up by their bootstraps. While that sounds inspiring, how exactly do you do that? Frankly, along with a good pair of boots with sturdy straps, you better have a plan and it better be a good one.

Now that you have read the above and concluded that you have the right stuff to be an entrepreneur, let's start with the mechanics of starting and operating your own business.

Creating a plan

· · · · · · · · · · · · · · · · · ·

Step 1: Write it down!

It starts with a business plan. You don't need to pay for a professionally done business plan unless you are applying for a loan from a bank. You need a written business plan mainly for yourself to help you keep focused on what you are trying to accomplish.

Running your own business requires focus and organization. Maybe you are that one in a million who can start and run a business by the seat of your pants, but I doubt it.

A good business plan always provides a solution to a problem. Your service or product must fill a need. Here is a simple outline for a do-it-yourself business plan:

1. **Company Summary** – What services and/ or products will your company provide? What business structure will you use (i.e., single proprietorship, partnership, corporation or Limited Liability Company)?

2. **Products and Services Summary** – Provide more detailed information about your proposed services and/or products. Why will your potential customers need your services and/or products? Who are your potential customers?

3. **Market Analysis Summary** – How did you determine who your potential customers will be? How do you intend to reach them?

4. **Implementation Summary** – Provide more detailed information on how you will develop your customer base. Can you can provide better services and/or products than your competition? How will you maintain your customer base?

5. **Management Summary** – Who will be managing/operating your company? What is their resume? How are they qualified to serve your company (this especially refers to yourself)?

6. **Financial Plan** – How will you obtain the financing to start and operate your company until it becomes profitable enough to pay you? Let's start with a projected monthly profit and loss statement.

Here is a basic outline for projecting a monthly profit and loss statement. (Your particular business may require more detail.)

Sample Profit and Loss Statement

Income (monthly gross)		**$12,345**
Expenses (monthly)		
Rent	$543	
Utilities	$234	
Telephone	$123	
Accounting	$45	
Legal	$22	
Dues and subscriptions	$12	
Salaries	$2,345	
Miscellaneous	$65	
Total Expense		**$3,389**
Profit or Loss *(income minus expenses)*		**$8,956**

You also need a written daily to-do list. Your list should begin with what you want to do the *least* followed in descending order to what you *most* want to do for the day. Do the worst task first. This will set the tone for the rest of the day. Don't spend your day delaying and fretting over something you don't want to do. Do it first and get it out of the way. This list should be updated every day. Each day should be a fresh list. A daily planner/calendar is essential.

Step 2: Establish yourself as an expert

If you don't have the knowledge or credentials to be an expert in the field of your new business, seek out the training that will give you the knowledge that will qualify you as an expert. Remember, there is no such thing as a part-time expert. You're either full-time or you're not an expert. Try to find a knowledgeable person in your field and ask them to mentor you.

Step 3: Select a location

Most brick-and-mortar stores are driven by their physical location. The wrong location will doom your business. The only exception to this is if your business will be done on the internet. In that case, your business can be located on your kitchen table or wherever your computer is located. If you are going to do business from your home, make sure the environment is free from distractions. If you want your business to be successful, treat it seriously.

Also, your smart phone or your notebook should serve as a portable office. I can access all three of my email accounts, my bank accounts, Skype and Facebook (both personal and business pages) from my smart phone.

Step 4: Financing your business

Do you have enough money saved to start and operate your business until it can support you? Cash is usually a big problem with a startup business. What is your cost to begin your business? What will your monthly operating expenses be? You must know these figures or your chances of success are low.

If you don't have the seed money, there are four alternatives for funding. The first is to borrow the money from a bank or lending institution. Frankly, unless you have discovered a cure for cancer, your chances of getting a loan for a startup business from a bank are slim and none, and Slim has left town. Usually the only way to obtain financing from a bank for a startup is by pledging other assets to guarantee the loan. If you have the assets to underwrite the loan, you better be sure you can live without those assets. I know more than one person who pledged their assets on a "can't miss" new business that somehow missed. They are still paying on the loan and the "can't miss" business is long gone.

The second source is to use your credit cards to provide the funding of your new business. Make sure you're willing to assume the risk of incurring this debt. "Can't miss" businesses miss all the time. Paying off maxed-out credit cards is a long range burden.

I had a "can't miss" business that missed. While reading airline magazines during various flights, I noticed a workout machine that claimed one could get a complete workout in four minutes. Finally, curiosity got the best of me and I checked out the manufacturer's website. Despite my original skepticism, I discovered considerable scientific studies which verified that the engineering of the machine did produce measurable results in four minutes a day, three days a week.

I made a trip to the factory that produced the machine and was thoroughly impressed with what I saw. The only catch with this product was its price tag of $15,000.00. Most people would not shell out that kind of money to put a machine in their house. But that was actually a plus for me.

I saw an opportunity. I felt that people would fall in love with the machine and the idea of getting fit in four minutes a day if they could go to a gym that offered the machine. I opened a location with three machines, and the gym quickly became a hit. Eventually, we expanded to three locations.

What a great idea! This has to be a "can't miss" business! Right? Not so fast, sweat sock breath! Gradually, our members grew tired of working out four minutes a day. Yes, tired of working out for *FOUR FREAKIN' MINUTES A DAY!* Our business dwindled down, in spite of me doing every promotion ever known to mankind. We finally had to shut our doors and go out of business. One of my partners made an astute observation after the fact. He said that we attracted people who didn't really want to work out to begin with.

MY "CAN'T MISS" BUSINESS MISSED!

The third source of outside financing is to borrow the money from a friend or family member. This is even more of a slippery slope. Your integrity and your intentions can be the best in the world, but if the business fails and the money is lost, your relationship with the friend or family member may be irrevocably damaged.

A fourth potential source is through a crowd-funding website like www.kickstarter.com. Crowd-funding is the practice of funding a project or venture by raising small amounts of money from a large number of people, usually via the internet. You can post your proposal for your new business with the amount of money you need to get started. If the members of the website feel you have a worthwhile project, they will contribute money to help you reach your goal.

Step 5: Set up a legal structure

If you are the only principal in your new business, you can operate as a single proprietorship, but you put your personal assets at risk if the business fails. For most people, setting up your business as a Limited Liability Company (LLC) is not only a professional way of doing business but also helps insulate your personal assets from a failure of your business. You do not have to pay someone to set this up for you. It is a simple process to set it up and register it with your state of residence. Go online to your particular state's website for the Secretary of State and register your new company as an LLC. Follow the simple prompts. The costs from state to state vary from $100 and up.

Step 6: Obtain a Tax Identification Number

Go to the IRS website www1.taxid-gov.us. By filling out the online form, you will get your federal TIN for your new LLC immediately and at no cost.

An LLC requires a tax return separate from your personal filings. Check with your Secretary of State for the tax filings that will be required.

Step 7: Set up a business bank account

This should be a different account from your personal account. If the business is solely owned by you and you operate as a sole proprietorship, you could do business out of your personal account, but it's much more professional to have a business account with your business name on the checks.

Step 8: Set up your website, email address and business card

In today's business arena, websites are not an option. You *must* have a website. You can set up your own website for a nominal monthly charge with sites such as GoDaddy (www.godaddy.com). GoDaddy offers inexpensive domain names, website hosting, website building and 24/7 customer support. I have used GoDaddy for many years and have been satisfied with them.

I have designed websites for half a dozen of my businesses. It is not hard to do, but my latest one, www. williamjoinerauthor.com, was designed by Andy Fincher. It is ten times better than any of my past websites that I designed myself. I would highly recommend Andy if you want a website that is professional and will pop out at your customers. You can reach Andy at andy@icopytexas.com. Andy is also my choice for business cards. Any project that I've ever thrown at him, he has hit out of the park.

Make sure you join Google+ (www.plus.google.com) and put a link to them on your website. Your website will have three times the visibility with search engines. The higher you're ranked with search engines, the better chance that someone can find you while looking for your service/ product on the internet.

Search engines such as Google and Yahoo are software systems designed to troll for information on the internet. Their secret algorithm will determine your ranking.

For your email platform, I would recommend www. yahoo.com or www.gmail.google.com. I have both. Both supply support and both are free.

Okay, that takes care of the preliminaries. Now it's time to roll up your sleeves and get to work!

Building
your business

. . . .

Who are you going to sell your product or service to? How do you determine who is your ideal customer? One of the great things about the internet is that you can find out whatever you want to know by doing a Google or Yahoo search.

A great way to find out about your potential customers is to Google/Yahoo search the subject of your business. If you're selling "thingamajigs," do a search for it. Your search will pull up a krillion (krillion is a bunch) companies that sell thingamajigs. Visit their websites and see what benefits their thingamajigs offer to their customers.

Please note there is a difference between a *benefit* and a *feature*. A feature of a vacuum cleaner may be portability. The *BENEFIT* is clean floors. Sell benefits, not features.

Study your competitors. Determine what you can do better than they can.

If your new company is offering a service instead of a product, it will be a little easier and cheaper to set up. An electrician may carry items to help service his customers, but he won't have to invest in an inventory of electrical fixtures. An electrical fixture store has to stock a complete selection of fixtures.

One exception to this is if your store is online, you may be able to take an order for a fixture and buy it from the wholesaler to be shipped directly to your customer. This is called drop-shipping. I had an online store that sold pepper spray. When someone ordered and paid me through my virtual store, I paid my wholesaler, who drop-shipped it directly to my customer. As a result, I didn't have to keep any pepper spray in my inventory.

Pricing

How are you going to price your thingamajigs? What is the competition selling them for? How many thingamajigs will you have to sell to break even before you can turn a profit? You have to know the answers to these questions.

There is a story of two hillbillies looking for a business opportunity. The first hillbilly said to the second hillbilly, "I figured it out, cuz! I knowed how we can make us a million dollars!"

The second hillbilly flashed a gap-toothed grin and responded, "How, cuz? Please tell me how!"

The first hillbilly tugged on his overalls and replied, "We gonna open us up an "all-you-can-eat" eatin' joint! And, we are only gonna charge 10 cents to eat! Everybody and their hound dog will eat there! We will make us a million!"

The second hillbilly scratched his head and his butt at the same time. "Well now, hold on, cuz. How we gonna make any money only charging folks a dime for all they can eat?"

The first hillbilly shouted and started to dance a jig. "Easy, cuz! We only gonna serve pig shit! Nobody can eat very much pig shit!"

It takes much more than numbers on a piece of paper to make a business successful.

Networking

Let's start building your network. What is a network and why is it important? A business network builds your business by providing contacts who will result in sales, or referring others who may become a customer for your product or services.

Your business network starts with your personal network, your family and friends. This can be tricky—you don't want your family and friends to start avoiding you to keep from being a victim of a sales pitch.

When I started in the insurance business, my office was the kitchen table in our home. Eventually, I owned or partnered in six agencies in six different locations in Texas.

Nobody likes an insurance agent trying to sell them insurance, but I started with my family and friends by asking for the opportunity to *SAVE THEM MONEY* on what they were currently spending on insurance. Being family and friends didn't mean they wanted to contribute financially for me to be a successful insurance agent, but most were dang sure interested in lowering their insurance premiums.

They didn't care about the features of the policy until they could see the benefit: *sending less money to the hated insurance companies.*

Your business network should include local organizations like the Chamber of Commerce, Lions Club, Kiwanis Club and any other civic-minded organizations. Your first priority should be to help the organizations, not sell your services or products. Don't go in as a taker but as a giver. Once you establish yourself as a valuable contributing member, the other members will take an interest in your business.

Can social media such as Facebook, Pinterest, LinkedIn and Twitter build your network? Absolutely—but you can't use social media just to pound and spam people about your business. It won't work that way because people will soon disconnect from you or tune you out. Before most people are going to be interested in what you have to say, they want to know if you're interested in what they have to say.

The social media that has given me the most traction is Facebook (www.facebook.com) for my book business www.williamjoinerauthor.com, and LinkedIn (www. linkedin.com) for my oil and gas business (www.joiner-petroleumservices.com). There is not enough time in the day to devote to more than one or two of the social media sites. After all, you have a business to run. Pick one, two at the most.

I had a Facebook page before I started writing books. I had already developed relationships based on personal interaction and exchanges. I had built up a following on Facebook by posting interesting and funny subject matter. A lot of these posts are about my life so people have gotten to know me. I'm not talking about mundane events (i.e., "I went to Walmart today and bought a toothbrush"). If my post is not getting enough interest with "likes," comments and shares, I delete it.

I began writing books because I was encouraged to do so by my Facebook contacts. My Facebook peeps have also been responsible for the bulk of my book sales, which is currently over 800 copies and counting. My first book was published in April 2014, the second in June 2014, the third in August 2014 and the fourth in November 2014. This book will be my fifth. I expect to publish it in late December 2014 or early January 2015.

Adding an additional Facebook page for business is easy. In fact, each of my books has its own Facebook page. I don't recommend Facebook ads to promote your business. I tried them and didn't get the results I wanted.

I established a large business network for my oil and gas business through LinkedIn, and it currently has over 1,500 LinkedIn connections. While I pursued connections initially, I no longer have to do that because my connection base now grows by 5-7 connections every week without me doing a thing but accepting connection requests from people who are interested in doing business with me. There are also groups on LinkedIn that you can join which share your particular area of business.

Unlike the other social media sites, LinkedIn is all about business. You can talk business as much as you want because personal chitchat is the exception, not the rule.

Trade shows are a great way to network. When I attended trade shows relating to the oil and gas business, I made many valuable contacts there. I am presently attending trade shows monthly to sell signed copies of my books and to expand my email list.

Selling

· · · · · · · · · ·

Selling your service or product is now your first order of business. If you don't have confidence in yourself when it comes to selling, you need to prepare and educate yourself to gain self-confidence. Your confidence is boosted by being prepared. Your prospective customer won't have the confidence to do business with you if you don't believe in yourself.

Here are some pointers in becoming a confident salesperson.

Ask questions

Once I hired a nationally-known sales consultant to give a seminar to the sales staff of one of my companies. He was terrific. He taught by *ASKING QUESTIONS!* He never stated any facts but pulled it out of my sales staff with his questions. My staff also retained his instruction because of the manner in which he taught by questioning them.

Asking questions is also a great way to approach a prospect and transition to a sale. The more that you know about your prospective customer, the better relationship and bond you can build with him. You definitely want your customers to bond with you. The more your customer talks, the better your chances of making a sale. Too many salespersons won't shut up long enough to listen to their customer.

Here are a list of questions a top salesperson might ask a potential customer.

- ✓ What is the biggest challenge for your company?
- ✓ What is your top priority?
- ✓ What do you like the most about your current service/product supplier?
- ✓ What would you change about your current supplier? (Do NOT criticize his current supplier)
- ✓ If you changed suppliers, what would you expect from your new supplier?
- ✓ What would it take to win your "Supplier of the Year" award?

Get referrals

Once you get your first sale, then comes a really important next step: *GET REFERRALS!* I understand that after your first sale, you just want to bask in the victory and perhaps dance a jig (remember the hillbilly) but referrals will be the life-blood of your company. The best lead you can have for a potential sale is the third-party endorsement that is a referral. *Not,* do you know anyone who would like all these fine features of my product, *but* do you know anyone who would also like the benefits of my product?

You won't get a referral from every one of your customers, but you need to ask every one of them. I can guarantee that you won't get referrals if you don't ask. You may want to provide an incentive for your customers for giving you a referral, such as 10% off on the next piece of business they do with you or a gift card. Referrals are business gold.

Testimonials

Ask your customer if they would give you a written testimonial that you could use on your website or in your advertising. Testimonials are a great way to promote your business. Some customers will be reluctant to go on record endorsing you, but you will have customers who will generously give you a testimony. You don't have to have a testimony from every customer, but if you ask for one from every customer, you will get enough to dramatically impact your business.

Also, it is helpful if you ask your customer why they bought from you. Again, the more you know about your customers, the better.

Help people

Our country is a capitalistic society, which is great because with capitalism comes opportunity. But there is a catch. You will not enjoy peace, joy and happiness from your business if you're strictly motivated by profit. Hopefully, you will also have a desire to help people. I don't mean a superficial, self-serving lip-service to help others which will result in you eventually being exposed as a fraud, but a deep-down desire to put another's welfare ahead of your own. Don't be like a lady who joined our church to sell Tupperware. When no one went to her sales event, she promptly quit our church declaring that we weren't friendly. There is great joy in helping others. If you truly desire to help people, the money will come to you.

Now that you have sales and customers, one of your customers contacts you about a problem with your service or product. How you handle complaints is crucial. Customer service can make or break your business. You need to do everything possible to address the problem immediately and make your customer happy. Nothing is stronger than word of mouth, pro and con. Also, return calls *promptly*. Nothing makes me madder than trying to do business with someone who won't communicate with me. In fact, once I experience a lack of communication twice, I am done with the company. I take my business elsewhere.

Advertising

. . . .

You will need a unique name for your company and a slogan or catch phrase that will tell the world who you are in a concise and clever manner. What? You're the world's greatest electrician but a name and a slogan stumps you? No problem! You can go to the website www.fiverr.com and choose from hundreds of talented writers and artists who will compete for the opportunity of naming your company or creating your slogan for a fee of $5. No, that is not a misprint. It really is *FIVE FREAKIN' DOLLARS!*

There are several different ways to advertise your new company. Different venues may work for different businesses. I never had any luck with radio, television, direct mail or the yellow pages.

The yellow pages is a mode of advertising that has come and gone. It is estimated that 90% of Americans now own a smart phone. If they're looking for services or products, they search the internet, not the yellow pages. That's why your business must be able to be found on the internet. You can hire a pay-per-click company like Google AdWords (www.google.com/adwords) to run internet ads for you.

You can set your own budget and you don't pay anything unless someone clicks on the ad which sends them to your website.

I do advertise with the local newspaper, the *Bridgeport Index*. It gives me a presence in the community, which is good for my business.

Cold-calling

Another way to get sales and build your network is "cold calling". This is when you call people you don't know to tell them about your service or product. Some salespersons are not comfortable doing this. They can't handle the rejection. I have done this on numerous occasions to boost sales for my companies. Maybe because I was born to be an entrepreneur, I am not offended by being ignored or dismissed in the business arena. If someone did that to me in my personal life it would lead to a confrontation, but I can separate personal from business. You must be able to handle rejection if you want to own your own business! You can also buy lists that pertain to your business for cold-calling purposes, but I prefer the local yellow pages.

Here is a possible script to cold-call. "Hello. Is the owner or the manager in? Mr. Owner, I'm Thenextbigthing Jones. Would you be interested in a great deal on thingamajigs if I can give you a better value than what you currently have? When would be a good time for me to come by to show you what I have?" Or, "May I send you my information on my thingamajigs?"

Cold-calling is not for the faint of heart or anyone lacking in the gonad department (sorry, ladies). Actually, some of the best cold-callers I've ever seen have been women. There's just something about a woman's voice over the telephone that will cause some men to take more time to listen. Yes, I know I can't be any more sexist than that, but that doesn't change the truth from being the truth.

I would also recommend you open a Skype account (www.skype.com). Skype will allow you to make telephone calls, domestic and out of the country, for a nominal fee. Video calls, group conference calls and file sharing are all included.

Email lists

More business gold comes from compiling an email list of people who do business with you or who are interested in doing business with you. You can entice them to join your list by offering monthly giveaways or special promotions. There should be a form on your website which allows visitors to sign up for your special offers. You can also collect applicants by individual contact. You just need their name and email address. I can't overemphasize how important a dynamic email list is for the growth of your new business.

A couple of cautions: First, don't send more than one email per month. Everyone hates to have their inbox flooded with emails. Second, don't spam (sending emails to people who didn't ask or agree to receive your email), as that is illegal. You're probably asking yourself: if spamming is so illegal, why do I get so much of it? Most spam originates from outside the United States, difficult to track down and prosecute. There are U.S. spammers, but they are playing a dangerous game.

It is not illegal to send mass emailings if the recipients have asked or agreed to receive emails from you. You can buy email lists from sources who guarantee the recipients have agreed to receive emails from companies such as yours. While not illegal, this is a waste of time. These lists have been sold hundreds, if not thousands, of times. The recipients have lost their patience by the time they receive a hundred emails from companies selling thingamajigs.

To keep from having to email everyone on your list individually, I suggest using a service that provides group mailings, like Constant Contact (www.constantcontact.com). Once you send an email to your list, Constant Contact will give you a report showing who opened your email and if there were any bounces due to faulty email addresses. Constant Contact has done a great job for me for years.

Online sales

. . . .

You can sell your products on the internet through not only your website but sales platforms like eBay (www.ebay.com) and Amazon (www.amazon.com).

If the product you are selling is digital, such as eBooks, downloadable music, internet television, digital subscriptions, internet coupons, software, mobile apps or cloud-based applications, you can sell your product through ClickBank (www.clickbank.com). ClickBank is a privately held online marketplace for digital information products. It aims to serve as a connection between digital content creators and affiliate marketers, who then promote them to consumers. If you have a good product at a good price, hundreds of affiliates would have an interest in selling your product for a commission.

You can take payments via credit cards on your website with PayPal (www.paypal.com). PayPal provides a secure way for your customers to pay, and you can also use it to invoice your customers. You can take credit card payments anywhere via your smart phone or tablet using Square (www.squareup.com) by downloading their app to your device. Square also provides a secure buying experience for your customer and will email them a receipt of the transaction.

Another way to increase sales is to partner up with an ancillary company that provides goods or services in your general field, but is not in competition with you. You can refer customers to each other in a mutually beneficial situation, such as an attorney and an accountant who refer their clients to each other.

Managing growth

. . . .

Hiring

Once you start to grow, your first impulse may be to get bigger. Bigger is not always better. Getting bigger usually means adding employees. The largest expense with most companies large or small is their payroll. Before you add an employee, you need to ask yourself if this additional employee will make you money. Every employee should be viewed as an income stream. An employee can free you to do what you do best, but if an employee will not make you money, don't hire them.

If and when you decide to hire an employee, it is paramount that you fully train them. Don't rely on "common sense." Don't assume that their common sense will direct them to choose the correct course of action regarding business matters.

Once I observed one of my employees assisting a customer when she answered an incoming call and dealt with the phone customer's problems while the customer in front of her had to wait until the phone call was finished. When she finished with both customers, I conducted an impromptu training session on customer protocol. I explained to her if she had a customer in the office and there was no one else to handle an incoming call, answer the phone, explain to the caller that she was currently tied up with helping another customer and politely ask the phone customer if she could call them back as soon as she was free. The customer in front of you takes precedence.

Who was at fault for this incident? Clearly, it was me for assuming my employee would know how to handle this particular situation. My fault was neglecting her training.

Also, you may want something done in a certain way that is not readily apparent to someone else. There is no substitute for good training.

Bookkeeping and taxes

The most economical way to keep your books and file your taxes is to do it yourself. You can do your own accounting with the Quick Books software (www.quickbooks.com). I have used them for years. With Quick Books you can keep an instant tab on your expenses and income, send invoices, pay bills, and manage employee payroll.

You can cheaply file your own taxes using Turbo Tax (www.turbotax.com). You don't have to be a trained accountant to use Turbo Tax. Just follow the step-by-step instructions in plain language. It will file your taxes electronically. I have also successfully used them.

I want to be clear on one thing. I am *NOT* advising you not to use a lawyer or a CPA. In most startup businesses, money is tight. As long as your situation is not complicated, you can save money by doing it yourself. When your business grows larger and more complicated, you will definitely need a good lawyer and CPA.

Insurance

You also need to determine whether your services or product needs business insurance. Ask a trusted insurance agent who specializes in business insurance but won't try to sell you a policy just to earn a commission. Your average insurance agent who sells life, health, home and auto insurance usually knows very little about business insurance. Find an expert.

Lawyers

I try to avoid the legal system but sometimes it can't be helped. Being in business for more than 45 years, I've gone to court on several occasions. You can be sued by *anyone* for *anything*.

I was once sued for a million dollars for alleged fraud on my part in the oil and gas business. The plaintiff claimed that I illegally took his oil and gas leases. Surely if someone sues another for a million dollars, there's got to be something to it, doesn't there? Where there's smoke, there has to be fire, right? The plaintiff managed some oil wells and leases that my partner and I owned. When we changed managers, he sued, claiming the leases were his. As ridiculous as it sounds, it would be the same as an apartment complex owner changing managers and the manager claiming that because he managed them, he owned the apartment complex. Of course we prevailed as we had no problem proving our ownership. The judge chewed out the opposing counsel for bringing a frivolous lawsuit into her court, but we were still out the cost of our attorney and the cost of our time.

I was sued another time by a man who bought one of my insurance agencies. Two years after he bought the agency, he sued me for fraud (fraud is a catch-all basis for any business lawsuit) alleging I misled him about the future profitability of the agency. He thought he was going to get bigger annual bonuses from the insurance companies that the agency represented. The bonuses are determined by an agency's loss ratios (how profitable your agency was to the insurance company). Any idiot should know you can't predict loss ratios—except this idiot. His current office manager (my old office manager) testified reluctantly that I had given her instructions, when he was evaluating the agency, to turn over any and all files to him, including clients and companies. One would think that the purpose of the suit would be to recover any losses he had sustained from buying the agency. Not so! The agency income had *increased* 10% every year since he purchased it. I won but still incurred the cost of going to arbitration. Again, *anyone* can sue for *anything!*

Sometimes you have no choice but to sue and pursue a legal remedy yourself. If the amount in question is less than $10,000, I recommend small claims court. You can sue someone without having to be represented by an attorney. You can file suit in a regular court without an attorney, but a real attorney will eat you alive in a regular court with his knowledge of the legal system. The cost of filing suit in small claims court is only a few hundred dollars.

I have had to sue twice and had excellent results. I was hired to do title work on oil and gas leases by a company in Oklahoma City. They refused to pay me and, as it turned out, about half a dozen other petroleum landmen claiming we had done substandard work. The problem was they refused to say what was substandard about my work. I finally had my fill of their stonewalling me, hoping I'd just go away. I filed suit in small claims court. Within two weeks after they were served with the notice of the suit, they paid me. I subsequently learned the other landmen got paid also. The other landmen were most appreciative of my efforts.

In the second case, I was having trouble with one of the major credit bureaus. They refused to delete a piece of erroneous bad credit on my report even after I sent them proof of the error. I (David) sued their asses (Goliath). Two of their attorneys showed up for the hearing. After hearing the evidence, the wise old justice of the peace told both parties to try to settle it, as one side was not going to like his ruling. He excused himself while we negotiated. Their lead attorney agreed to delete the information and we settled. She told me she wished she had been fully apprised of the situation. It would have saved them a trip to Bridgeport, Texas. About a month later, I called the main number of the credit bureau to tell her of my appreciation for her help in resolving the matter. I fully expected to get an operator and ask for the attorney. Instead, my call was routed directly to the attorney's office, bypassing the switchboard. Sometimes, when you stand up for yourself, you earn respect.

Your personal life

· ·

In closing, I want to give some advice about your personal life. Some might think that your personal life is none of my business, and they would be right. But I'm going to do it anyway.

Be careful of the company you keep. Hang out with positive, encouraging people. Negative people will drain you of your energy and influence your outlook on life for the worse. There is truth in the old saying, "a rotten apple spoils the barrel."

My relationship with God is the most important thing in my life. My family is blessed through that relationship. My business is blessed through that relationship.

Your business should be a reflection of who you are as a person. My morals and ethics are the same whether it's in my personal life or my business life. I am far from perfect but I try to walk my talk. My dad always said that a man is no better than his word. My integrity is far more important to me than making money.

Regardless whether I am going through an up period or a down period, I try to always be grateful to God for my blessings.

You are now ready to get on the roller coaster ride that is *owning your own business*. I wish you the best. If you need further help, I am available for consultation. Contact me for my rates at:

williamjoinerauthor@gmail.com

DISCLAIMER

The information contained in this book is for general guidance on matters of interest only. The application and impact of laws can vary widely based on the specific facts involved. Given the changing nature of laws, rules and regulations, there may be omissions or inaccuracies contained in this book. Accordingly, the information in this book is provided with the understanding that the author and publisher are not herein engaged in rendering legal, accounting, tax, or other professional advice and services. As such, it should not be used as a substitute for consultation with professional accounting, tax, legal or other competent advisers. Before making any decision or taking any action, you should consult such professionals.

ACKNOWLEDGEMENTS

I am grateful for the constant support of my wife, Tina, and my children: Jacob, Caleb, Sarah and Ainslee.

Thank you to Missy Brewer for editing this book, to Michael Campbell for the book design, and to Bryan Gehrke for the cover artwork.

William Joiner can be contacted at:

williamjoinerauthor@gmail.com

Learn more at

www.williamjoinerauthor.com

Joining the Rewards Club on my website is 100% FREE and scores you a FREE eBook copy of *American Entrepreneur*. As a Rewards Club member you will receive monthly notices of future giveaways and special promotions. My pledge to you is you won't receive an email from me more than once a month.

www.williamjoinerauthor.com

www.ingramcontent.com/pod-product-compliance
Lightning Source LLC
Chambersburg PA
CBHW021040180526
45163CB00005B/2219